Taste The Vinoy

"Without Reservations"

Espichel Enterprises / Publishers

RENAISSANCE
VINOY
RESORT AND
GOLF CLUB

ST. PETERSBURG, FLORIDA

The Vinoy has been a St. Petersburg landmark since it opened in 1925 as the winter playground for the rich and famous.

Today the resort includes an 18-hole golf course and clubhouse, a tennis complex, pools, day spa, fitness center and a 74-slip marina.

The recipes in this book are from dishes featured at the Vinoy's five superior restaurants, from poolside casual at Alfresco's to the elegant cuisine of Marchand's Bar & Grill.

They are favorites of Executive Chef John Pivar, Executive Sous Chef Mark Heimann, Pastry Chef Bill Hallion and Banquet Chef James Samson.

Executive Chef John Pivar

Welcome to the Vinoy

The Vinoy has been a symbol of "Simple Elegance" from its very beginning some eight decades ago. After several renovations to restore its Mediterranean grandeur, that spirit of the times is still present in its architecture and service, and most importantly - in our cuisine.

In each of our five restaurants we offer menus to satisfy a variety of tastes with dishes that are "simply elegant" using only the highest quality of products from the freshest produce and seafood to the best aged beef. The following recipes, from appetizers to desserts, will offer you the opportunity to create our favorite and most requested dishes at home. We have also included a "simply elegant" seven course dinner for eight which we prepare at the Vinoy for our very special guests. We sincerely hope you enjoy Taste The Vinoy "Without Reservations".

John Pivar

Beginnings

Butternut Bisque

Seafood Chowder

Crab Cakes

Three Flatbreads

Hummus

Gorgonzola Tart

Tomato Mozzarrella Stack

Artichoke Salad

8

Butternut Squash Bisque

 Serves eight

3 butternut squash, halved and seeded
2 tsps cinnamon
1 tsp nutmeg
1/2 cup honey
3/4 stick butter
1/4 cup diced celery
1/4 cup diced carrot
1/2 cup diced onion

2 garlic cloves
2 cups heavy cream
salt and pepper to taste
4 tblsps creme fraiche

Cinnamon Sugar Croutons
1 cup diced white bread
1/2 stick butter, melted
1 tblsp mixture of cinnamon and sugar

Sprinkle squash with cinnamon and nutmeg and drizzle with honey. Cube 1/2 stick butter and divide between the squash halves. Cover with plastic and foil and bake at 350° for 1-1/2 hours until soft. Cool and scoop the pulp from the skins.
In a 4 quart sauce pot, sweat the celery, carrot, onion and garlic in the remaining 1/4 stick of butter. Add the squash pulp, cover with water and simmer for 1/2 hour. Remove from heat and puree. Add the heavy cream, bring to a boil and season to taste. To serve, top with croutons and drizzle with creme fraiche.

For Cinnamon Sugar Croutons: Mix all ingredients together and toast on a cookie sheet until light brown.

Enjoy specialty sandwiches, salads and soups like this Seafood Chowder in the casual poolside atmosphere of Alfresco's.

Seafood Chowder

 Serves eight

1 tblsp unsalted butter
1/4 white onion, diced
1/2 green pepper, diced
2 garlic cloves, minced
1/4 tsp curry powder
1/4 tsp jerk seasoning
1/2 tsp fresh chopped thyme
2 cups V-8 juice
2 cups chopped clams with juice

2 cups clam juice
1/2 tomato, diced
1/2 cup diced potatoes
1/2 orange, zested and juiced
3/4 lb grouper, diced into 1" pieces
1 cup heavy cream
2-1/2 tblsps cornstarch
salt and pepper to taste
2 scallions, chopped

Heat the butter in a large soup pot over medium heat and saute the onion, pepper, garlic and curry powder for 4 minutes. Stir in jerk seasoning, thyme and cook for 1 minute. Add the V-8 juice, chopped clams, clam juice, tomato, potato, orange zest, juice and season to taste. Bring to a boil, lower to a simmer and cook uncovered for approximately 15 minutes. Add the grouper and cook until just opaque and flaky, about 3 to 4 minutes. In a separate bowl, whip the cornstarch into the cream, then stir into the soup. Simmer for 5 more minutes. Season to taste and stir in scallions to finish. Serve and garnish with toasted tortilla strips.

These light and delicious crab cakes are a favorite at the Vinoy Clubhouse. Enjoy them after playing 18 holes on the newly restored golf course!

Jumbo Lump Crab Cakes

 Serves four

1 lb jumbo lump crabmeat
2 scallions, chopped
1 egg, beaten
1/4 red bell pepper, diced small
1 tsp cumin
pinch cayenne pepper

3 tblsps mayonnaise
2 tblsps whole grain mustard
1/4 cup Japanese bread crumbs
1 tblsp whole butter
1 tblsp vegetable oil
salt and pepper to taste

Check for shells by gently sifting through crabmeat. Add scallions, egg, diced pepper, cumin, cayenne, mayonnaise and mustard. Toss thoroughly and gently, making sure not to break up the crabmeat lumps as much as possible. Season with salt and pepper to taste. Divide into eight portions and roll in bread crumbs. Heat butter and oil over medium heat and sear cakes for 2 minutes on each side or until golden brown and warm inside.

Flatbreads

Serves six

3 pizza dough balls, 3 oz each
cornmeal, for dusting

Roll each ball out into very thin ovals, 4" x 10". Place on a cookie sheet dusted with cornmeal and top each with one of the following mixtures. Bake at 450° for 10 to 12 minutes until golden and crispy. Slice and serve.

Lobster and Wild Mushrooms
2 tblsps pesto sauce
1/4 cup shredded fontina cheese
4 shiitake mushrooms, julienned
1 tblsp olive oil
4 oz cooked Maine lobster meat, chopped

Saute mushrooms in oil. Brush dough with pesto sauce and top with cheese, mushrooms and lobster.

Spinach, Pear and Gorgonzola Cheese
1-1/2 tblsps olive oil
1/4 anjou pear
1/2 cup fresh spinach
1/4 cup gorgonzola cheese
2 tblsps chopped walnuts

Peel, core and slice pear. Brush dough with oil and top with pear, spinach, cheese and walnuts.

Lamb, Feta Cheese and Herbs
1 lamb loin, 6 oz
salt and pepper to taste
1 tblsp mixed chopped oregano and parsley
1 garlic clove, minced
3 tblsps crumbled feta cheese
2 tblsps julienned red onion
6 grape tomatoes, halved

Tzatziki Sauce
4 tblsps plain yogurt
1/4 seedless cucumber, diced
juice of 1/2 lemon
2 tsps chopped fresh dill
1/2 tsp minced garlic
salt and pepper to taste

Season lamb and sear until medium rare. Brush dough with oil and top with remaining ingredients. Bake, then top with sliced lamb and drizzle with tzatziki sauce.
For Tzatziki Sauce: Puree first five ingredients together and season to taste.

Hummus

 Serves four

16 oz can garbanzo beans
fresh squeezed juice of 1 lemon
2 garlic cloves, minced
1 tblsp tahini
salt and white pepper to taste
1 roasted red pepper
10 kalamata olives
2 tblsps crumbled feta cheese
2 slices pita bread
olive oil

Maintain your fitness regimen at the Vinoy Health Club, complemented by healthy cuisine such as this hummus recipe. Enjoy it at our popular Mediterranean Sunday Brunch.

Drain and puree the garbanzo beans. Add the lemon juice, garlic and tahini. Mix well and season with salt and white pepper. Divide into three equal portions.

Dice half of the red pepper and puree the other half. Blend in well with one of the three portions.

Drain and finely dice the olives. Blend in well with the feta cheese into the third portion.

Brush the pita bread with olive oil and grill. Slice each into eight pieces and serve with the three flavors of hummus.

Pineapple & Gorgonzola Cheese Cakes

 Serves four

1/4 cup gorgonzola cheese
1/2 cup cream cheese
2 eggs
1/4 cup heavy cream
4 tblsps pineapple, diced small
salt and white pepper to taste
4 prebaked 3-1/2" tart shells
2 cups mixed baby greens

**Sundried Tomato &
Truffle Oil Vinaigrette**

1/4 cup sundried tomatoes
1/4 cup rice wine vinegar
1 egg yolk
3/4 cup canola oil
1 tsp truffle oil
2 tsps water
salt & pepper to taste

Soften cheeses, then whip with a mixer until smooth. Add eggs and mix until creamy. Add cream, mix until well combined and season with salt and pepper. Place the pineapple in the bottom of each shell. Add excess pineapple juice to cheese batter and mix well. Pour the batter in the shells and bake at 350° for 15 to 17 minutes until the eggs have set. Let cool.

For Vinaigrette: Chop tomatoes and puree with vinegar and egg yolk in food processor. Drizzle in canola and truffle oils. Adjust thickness with water and season to taste.

Parmesan Grissini Sticks

1 egg, beaten
2 tblsps heavy cream
1/4 cup grated parmesan cheese
4 grissini sticks
   (small, hard bread sticks)

Combine the egg and cream and brush onto each stick. Roll sticks in cheese and bake on a greased cookie sheet at 350° for 6 minutes or until light brown.

Tomato Mozzarella Stack

 Serves four

4 ripe tomatoes
8 oz fresh mozzarella cheese
20 large fresh basil leaves
4 small bunches fresh mache
4 tblsps extra virgin olive oil
4 tblsps balsamic glaze
salt & pepper to taste

Guests can enjoy quiet conversations over private lunch or cocktails in picturesque settings that abound at the Vinoy.

Core the tomato necks and score the bottoms. Submerge tomatoes in boiling water for 30 seconds. Remove from heat and shock in ice water to chill. Remove the skin from the tomatoes.
Slice the tomatoes and mozzarella in 1/4" slices. Alternate tomato, cheese, basil leaf, salt and pepper until you have a stack five tomato slices high.
Serve each stack with a small bunch of mache. Drizzle tomato stacks and greens with olive oil. Decorate plates with balsamic glaze.

Baby Artichoke Arugula Salad

 Serves four

16 baby artichokes
2 roasted red peppers, julienned
2 roasted yellow peppers, julienned
1/2 medium red onion, julienned
4 cups arugula
5 oz goat cheese, crumbled
salt and pepper to taste
2 shallots, sliced thin
vegetable oil for frying

Citrus Dressing
2 tblsps rice wine vinegar
juice of 1/2 lemon
juice of 1/2 lime
juice of 1 orange
1 tblsp dijon mustard
1 egg yolk
1/2 shallot, minced
1 cup vegetable oil
salt and pepper to taste

Clean, peel and blanch artichokes in boiling water. Remove and place on a bed of ice to chill. Cut in half and remove the fuzzy choke. Mix with peppers in a large bowl. Add onion, arugula and half of the goat cheese. Pour the citrus dressing over, season and mix well. Fry the shallots in very hot oil until crisp and place on top of the salad with remaining goat cheese.

For Citrus Dressing: Puree the first seven ingredients together. Drizzle in oil while continuing to puree, then add salt and pepper to taste.

Seafood

Bouillabaisse

Paella

Teriyaki Tuna

Nut Crusted Grouper

Crispy Yellowtail

Salmon Stack

Salmon Salad

Mizo Glazed Seabass

Bouillabaisse

 Serves four

2 tblsps extra virgin olive oil
1 tblsp chopped garlic
1 tblsp chopped shallots
8 medium littleneck clams, cleaned
2 yukon gold potatoes, diced
1/4 cup white wine
2 tblsps saffron threads
8 large scallops
8 mussels, cleaned
8 large shrimp, peeled and deveined
8 oz cubed fish (white or salmon)
2 lobster tails, 8 oz each, split in half
4 cups fish stock (or canned clam juice)
1 stick butter, cubed
salt & pepper to taste
1 tomato, chopped

4 slices ciabatta bread
2 tblsps extra virgin olive oil
1 tblsp chopped garlic

Sweat garlic and shallots in oil over medium heat until shallots are clear. Add clams, potatoes, wine and saffron. Reduce until wine is almost gone. Add scallops, mussels and shrimp, season to taste and cook for two minutes. Season fish with salt and pepper, then add with lobster to the pan. Pour in fish stock and season to taste. Simmer until shrimp are pink. Add butter and heat until melted. Brush bread slices with oil and garlic and grill or broil until light brown. Spoon bouillabaisse into bowls, garnish with chopped tomatoes and serve with half slices of toasted bread.

Vinoy's Paella

 Serves two

4 oz chistora (Spanish summer sausage)
2 tsps chopped garlic
1/2 cup chopped onions
6 oz boneless chicken, cut into 1-1/2" strips
3 oz boneless pork, diced into 1/2" pieces
1-3/4 cups uncooked rice
1-1/2 tblsps saffron threads
4-1/2 cups chicken stock (or canned broth)
6 pieces escargot
4 cherrystone clams
4 black mussels, cleaned
4 large shrimp, peeled and deveined
1-1/4 lb lobster, split and cleaned
3 tblsps chopped green and red peppers
3 tblsps diced tomatoes
1/4 cup frozen green peas

2 tblsps extra virgin olive oil
1/4 cup white wine
salt and pepper to taste

Roll sausage into balls and saute over medium heat until light brown. Add garlic and onions, saute until onions are clear, stirring occasionally. Add chicken, pork and cook until light brown. Stir in rice and mix well. Add saffron, 4 cups of stock and season with salt and pepper. Cover and simmer about 20 minutes until rice is half cooked. Add escargot, mussels and clams, cover and cook 4 minutes until mussels and clams begin to open. Add shrimp, lobster, peppers, tomatoes and remaining 1/2 cup stock. Cover and cook until shrimp are pink. Sprinkle with peas and cook until peas are thawed. Pour into a large 2 quart serving bowl and drizzle with olive oil and wine.

Teriyaki Glazed Yellowfin Tuna

 Serves four

Teriyaki Glaze
1/2 cup sake
1/4 cup soy sauce
1/2 cup sugar

Wasabi Butter
1-1/2 tblsps wasabi powder
1/4 cup white wine
3 tblsps heavy cream
1 stick butter, softened
salt and pepper to taste

4 yellowfin tuna loins, 6 oz each,
    2" x 2" x 4" barrel cut
1 tblsp sesame oil
salt and pepper to taste
1/2 cup chow mein noodles, fried

Season loins and sear in oil for 1 minute on each side for rare. Brush with teriyaki glaze and serve with stir fried vegetables over noodles and wasabi butter.

For Teriyaki Glaze: Combine all ingredients in a sauce pot and bring to a boil. Reduce heat to a simmer and cook until thick. Let cool.

For Wasabi Butter: Heat the wasabi powder and wine in a sauce pot and reduce until almost dry. Add the cream and simmer for 30 seconds. Reduce heat and slowly whisk in butter. Season with salt and pepper.

Stir Fried Vegetables
1 cup chiffonade bok choy
6 shiitake mushrooms
1/2 cup bean sprouts
1/4 cup thinly sliced carrots
1/4 red pepper, julienned
1/4 yellow pepper, julienned
1/2 cup cut snow peas
1 tblsp sesame oil

Stir fry vegetables in sesame oil until half cooked. Add 1 tblsp teriyaki glaze and cook until vegetables are crisp tender.

Macadamia Nut Crusted Grouper

The Vinoy is a favorite port-of-call, not only for its great facilities, but also for the superb seafood served at each of its five restaurants.

 Serves four

4 grouper fillets, 5 oz each
3/4 cup macadamia nuts
1/4 cup Japanese bread crumbs
1/4 cup flour
2 eggs, beaten
3 tblsps canola oil
salt & pepper to taste
4 cups fresh pea shoots (or spinach)
1 tblsp butter
1-1/2 cups candied ginger sticky rice

Papaya Salsa
1/2 ripe papaya, peeled and seeded
1/2 tomato
1/4 red onion
1/2 tblsp chopped cilantro
2 tblsps orange juice
1 tsp red wine vinegar
1 tsp canola oil
salt & pepper to taste

For Papaya Salsa: Dice the papaya, tomato and onion and mix with the remaining ingredients. Salt and pepper to taste.

In a food processor, pulse nuts and bread crumbs together until chunky. Season to taste. Salt and pepper fillets to taste and lightly flour. Shake off excess flour and dredge in eggs. Press the nut and bread crumb mixture onto the fillets. Over medium high heat, saute fillets in hot oil for 2 minutes on each side. Meanwhile, saute the pea shoots in butter, season to taste and cook until wilted. Spoon shoots over candied ginger sticky rice, top with a fillet and serve with the salsa.

Crispy Yellowtail Snapper

 Serves four

4 snapper fillets, 5 oz each
1/2 cup cornstarch
salt and pepper to taste
1 cup vegetable oil
1/4 cup diced cantaloupe
1/4 cup diced honeydew
1/4 cup diced watermelon
2 tblsps chiffonade mint
2 tblsps honey
1/2 cup fried plantains

Smoked Orange Butter Sauce
4 oranges, halved
hickory wood chips, soaked in water
1 shallot, minced
1/4 cup white wine
3 tblsps heavy cream
1 stick butter, softened
salt and pepper to taste

Molasses Rum Syrup
1/4 cup dark rum
1 tblsp fresh ginger
1/3 cup molasses

For Orange Butter Sauce: On an outdoor grill, smoke oranges for 10 minutes, cut side up, once the chips begin to smoke. Squeeze orange juice into a heated sauce pot with shallot and wine and reduce until almost dry. Add cream and cook 30 seconds. Remove from heat, whisk in butter and season.

For Molasses Rum Syrup: Cook rum and ginger together and reduce until almost dry. Add molasses and simmer for 1 minute. Remove from heat.

Make a salsa by combining the diced melons with the mint and honey. Salt and pepper to taste. Score the skin on each fillet. Mix cornstarch with salt and pepper, then pat onto fillets. Shallow fry in hot oil, skin side down first. Fry on each side for 3 to 4 minutes, remove and pat dry with paper towels. Serve the fillets over the salsa, top with fried plantains and drizzle the plates with smoked orange butter sauce and molasses rum syrup.

Pan Roasted Salmon Stack

 Serves four

8 salmon fillets, 3 oz each
2 russet potatoes, shredded
2 tblsps extra virgin olive oil
8 oz hearts of palm
2 tblsps whole butter
2 tsps chopped garlic
4 cups fresh spinach
1/4 cup sundried tomatoes, julienned
1/2 round of boursin cheese
salt & pepper to taste

Puree:
1/4 cup sundried tomatoes
1/4 cup extra virgin olive oil
pinch of chopped garlic
1/4 cup water

Divide potatoes into 8 thin round portions and saute in a hot skillet coated with oil until crispy. Set aside.

Split hearts of palms in half lengthwise, season with salt and pepper, then saute in butter until golden brown. Set aside.

For Puree: Puree tomatoes, garlic and oil together. Add water and puree until smooth. Sweat garlic in olive oil, add spinach, tomatoes and cook until spinach is wilted. Stir in the cheese, mix well and set aside.

Season salmon with salt and pepper, then sear in a hot skillet coated with oil for 2-1/2 minutes on each side.

Build a "stack" by layering hearts of palm, salmon fillet, spinach mixture, followed by a potato crisp. Continue to build with another salmon fillet, spinach mixture and a second potato crisp. Drizzle puree around plate.

Mango Ginger Glazed Salmon Salad

 Serves four

4 salmon fillets, 5 oz each
1/2 each red & yellow pepper, julienned
1 cup mandarin orange sections
1 European cucumber, ribbon sliced
6 cups mixed baby greens
1 ripe mango, pureed
1 tblsp grated fresh ginger
1/4 cup toasted slivered almonds
olive oil, salt & pepper to taste

Maple Dressing:
1/4 cup mayonnaise
1/4 cup pure maple syrup
1-1/2 tblsps champagne vinegar
1 tsp white sugar
3 tblsps vegetable oil

Brush salmon fillets with olive oil and season with salt and pepper. Place on hot grill and cook for two minutes on each side. Combine pureed mango with ginger and brush glaze on fillets. Cook on grill for one minute. Divide mixed greens and peppers into 4 bundles and roll each tightly with a cucumber ribbon. Place each bundle on a plate with a salmon fillet and scatter with mandarin orange sections. Drizzle maple dressing over greens. Garnish plate with additional mango ginger glaze and sprinkle with almond slivers.

For Maple Dressing:
In a medium bowl, whisk together mayonnaise, syrup, vinegar and sugar. Gradually whisk in vegetable oil. Salt and pepper to taste.

Miso Glazed Seabass With Sushi Roll

 Serves four

4 seabass fillets, 5 oz each
2 tblsps miso paste
1 tlbsp honey
2 tblsps mirin (sweet cooking rice wine)
3 tblsps canola oil
4 tblsps sweet soy sauce

Vegetable Sushi Roll
1 cup uncooked Japanese sticky rice
2 cups water
1 carrot
1 European cucumber
1 red pepper
1 handful pea trendrils or sprouts
4 sheets nori, 4" x 6"
1/2 cup toasted peanuts, chopped

Mix miso paste, honey and mirin and rub onto fillets. Over medium high heat, saute fillets in oil for 2 minutes on each side.

Cook rice in water for 20 minutes at a very low heat so that it steams (using a rice cooker is best). Julienne the carrot, cucumber and pepper, cutting the carrot and cucumber into 6 inch slices. Using a sushi mat, form a quarter of the rice into a 4" x 6" rectangle. Top with a sheet of nori, add the vegetables and roll tightly. Repeat to make 3 more rolls. Roll in toasted peanuts. Serve the seabass with sliced sushi roll and drizzle with sweet soy sauce.

Poultry

Stuffed Chicken Breasts

Chicken Oscar

Pecan Chicken

Chicken & Pasta

Maple Duck Breasts

Roasted Game Hen

Stuffed Breast of Chicken

 Serves four

4 boneless chicken breasts, 8 oz each, with skin
3 tblsps olive oil
3 cups fresh spinach, chopped
1/4 cup toasted pine nuts
1 whole Boursin cheese wheel
salt & pepper to taste

Marsala Raisin Sauce
1 shallot, minced
1/4 cup golden raisins
1/2 cup Marsala wine
1 cup demi glace
1 tblsp butter

Mix the spinach with the pine nuts and cheese and season to taste. Stuff the spinach mixture under the skin on the breasts, season with salt and pepper to taste. Preheat the oil in an oven proof skillet until very hot. Place the breasts skin side down and sear for 3 to 4 minutes until golden brown. Flip the breasts over and finish in a 350° oven for 15 to 18 minutes or until cooked through.

For Marsala Raisin Sauce: Cook shallot, raisins and wine in a saute pan over medium high heat and reduce until almost dry. Add demi glace, reduce to a simmer and cook for 10 minutes. Salt and pepper to taste, remove from heat and add butter. Spoon Marsala raisin sauce on the plate.

Chef's Suggestion: Serve with steamed pencil asparagus and sweet potato pave.

Chicken Oscar

 Serves four

4 chicken breasts, 4 oz each
20 asparagus spears
1/4 cup light tempura mix

2 cups vegetable or peanut oil
2 red tomatoes

Halve and pound the chicken breasts until thin and grill for 4 to 5 miniutes. Cut the tomatoes into 1/4" slices and grill for 2 to 3 minutes. Cut off the woody ends and halve the asparagus spears. Arrange on skewers in groups of five, dip in tempura batter and deep fry in oil until crisp. Remove and drain. Make a "stack" starting with a tomato slice, followed by a chicken breast, asparagus spear and choron hollandaisse. Repeat layers and finish with a topping of crabmeat.

Choron Hollandaisse
1/2 lb lump crabmeat
1 tomato, diced
1 tsp chopped tarragon
1/2 tsp chopped parsley

1 shallot, minced
1/4 cup white wine
2 egg yolks
1-1/2 sticks butter, melted
salt and pepper to taste

Cook tomato, herbs, shallot and wine until reduced to a paste. Over a double boiler, whip the egg yolks and tomato reduction together until the yolks are steaming. Remove from heat and slowly add the butter while whipping. Season to taste and stir in the crabmeat.

Pecan Chicken with Creamy Succotash

 Serves four

6 chicken breasts, 4 oz each, split
1/2 cup pecans
3 tblsps bread crumbs
1/2 tsp ground black pepper
1/2 tsp cayenne

1 tsp paprika
1/4 cup flour
2 eggs, beaten
1/4 cup vegetable oil
salt and pepper to taste

Combine pecans, bread crumbs, pepper, cayenne, paprika and chop in a food processor. Salt and pepper to taste. Lightly flour chicken breasts, dredge in egg wash, then coat with the pecan crumb mixture. Saute in oil for 2 minutes on each side, then finish in a 350° oven for 4 to 6 minutes. Serve with creamy succotash.

Creamy Succotash
3 slices of bacon, diced
1/4 cup pearl onions
2 garlic cloves, minced
kernels from 1 fresh ear of corn
1/4 cup lima beans

1/4 cup green beans, cut in 1" slices
1/2 tomato, seeded and diced
1/4 cup heavy cream
1 tsp chopped fresh thyme
salt and pepper to taste

Render the bacon until brown, remove and set aside. Add the onions and garlic to the bacon grease and cook for 1 minute. Stir in the corn, limas, green beans, tomatoes and cook for 30 seconds. Add heavy cream, thyme, season to taste and cook for an additional minute until thick. Stir in bacon and mix well.

Chef's Suggestion: Serve with sweet potato spoon bread.

Grilled Chicken Breasts
with Pappardelle

 Serves four

4 boneless, skinless chicken breasts, 4 oz each
4 portobello mushroom caps, cleaned, stems removed
6 each red and yellow grape tomatoes, halved
1/4 cup olive oil
2 tblsps chopped fresh thyme
2 tblsps chopped fresh basil
2 garlic cloves, chopped

1/2 tblsp cracked black pepper
salt to taste
2 cups fresh swiss chard, chiffonade
3 tblsps whole butter
1 garlic clove, chopped
4 oz pappardelle pasta, cooked al dente
2 tblsps pesto sauce

Coat the chicken breasts, mushroom caps and grape tomatoes with a mixture of olive oil, thyme, basil, garlic, and pepper. Season with salt. Place the mushroom caps and tomatoes on a rack and roast for 20 minutes in a 300° oven. Grill the breasts for 3 to 4 minutes on each side. Saute the swiss chard in butter with the garlic until just wilted. Toss the pasta in the garlic and thyme cream sauce. Make a "stack" starting with the mushroom cap, followed by the pasta and swiss chard. Top with the chicken breasts and garnish plates with pesto sauce. Or you may julienne the chicken breasts and mushroom caps and toss all ingredients together in the cream sauce.

Roasted Garlic and Thyme Cream Sauce
5 roasted garlic cloves, sliced
1/2 shallot, minced
1/2 cup white wine

1 cup heavy cream
1/4 cup grated asiago cheese
2 tsps chopped fresh thyme
salt and pepper to taste

In a sauce pot, simmer garlic and shallot in wine and reduce until almost dry. Add cream and cheese, then heat until cheese melts. Add thyme and season to taste.

Maple Glazed Duck Breasts

 Serves four

4 duck breasts, 5 oz each
1/4 cup maple syrup
salt and cracked black pepper to taste

Combine maple syrup, salt and pepper and rub onto breasts. Sear breasts, fat side down first, for 3 to 4 minutes on each side until caramelized and fat is rendered. Remove from heat, drain and pat dry with paper towels. Serve with potato rosti.

Potato Rosti

4 russett potatoes, unpeeled	1 tblsp butter, melted
1/2 onion, grated	1/4 cup clarified butter
2 tsps chopped fresh thyme	salt and pepper to taste

Shred the potatoes and squeeze out excess water. Add onions, thyme and combine well. Season to taste with salt and pepper. Place the potatoes in melted butter in a 6" oven proof pan and press firmly. Over medium high heat, cook until golden brown on bottom. Cover with a plate, flip and return to pan. Top with clarified butter and cook for 2 minutes. Finish by cooking in a 350° oven for 20 minutes until golden brown on top.

Chef's Suggestion: Serve with fresh seasonal vegetable bundles.

Roasted Game Hen with Applejack Foie Gras Demi Glace

Serves four

2 game hens, 1 lb each	1 red delicious apple, skinned, diced small
salt and pepper to taste	1 tblsp butter
1 cup demi glace	1/4 cup Applejack brandy
4 oz foie gras, diced	1/4 cup light brown sugar

Saute the foie gras and strain, reserving the oil. In a separate pot, heat the demi glace, then blend the foie gras oil in with a mixer. Add the cooked foie gras. Saute the apple briefly in butter, add the brandy and reduce by half. Add the sugar and heat until dissolved. Pour into the demi foie gras mixture and blend well.

Season the hens with salt and pepper and roast at 350° for 10 minutes. Chill then remove the rib, thigh and wish bones. In a hot skillet, saute hens skin side down until golden brown. Cook for 5 to 6 minutes at 350°. Serve with butternut squash, wilted spinach and drizzle with demi glace.

Butternut Squash	1/2 cup honey
2 butternut squash, halved and seeded	1/2 stick butter
2 tsps cinnamon	1/2 cup heavy cream
1 tsp nutmeg	salt and pepper to taste

Sprinkle squash with cinnamon and nutmeg and drizzle with honey. Cube the butter and divide between the squash halves. Cover with plastic and foil and bake at 350° for 1-1/2 hours until soft. Cool, scoop the pulp from the skins and puree. In a sauce pot, heat the squash puree with the heavy cream and season to taste.

Wilted Spinach	
4 cups fresh baby spinach	1 tsp chopped garlic
2 tblsps butter	salt and pepper to taste

Saute the spinach and garlic in melted butter until just wilted. Salt and pepper to taste.

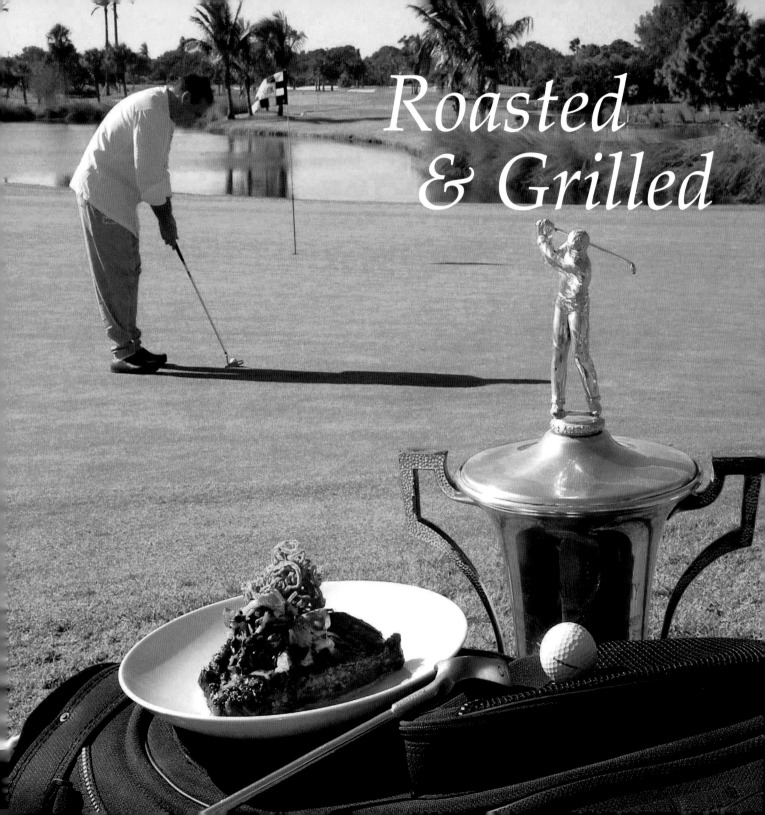

Roasted & Grilled

Beef Tenderloin

Short Ribs

Strip Steak

Flank Steak

Pork Roast

Pork Tenderloin

Veal T-Bones

Lamb Chops

Serves four

2 lbs beef tenderloin
olive oil
salt and pepper to taste

Beef Tenderloin

Season tenderloin and sear in hot oil on all sides for a total of 4 minutes. Finish in a 350° oven for 20 to 25 minutes. Remove at an internal temperature of 120° and let rest 10 minutes before slicing. Create a tower by filling half of a 3″ circular mold with the macaroni and cheese. Fill the remaining half with mashed broccoli and top with a dollop of tomato fondue.

Black Truffle Macaroni and Cheese

2 tblsps butter	1 tblsp chopped black truffles
2 tblsps flour	1 egg, beaten
1 cup scalded milk	1/4 lb ditalini, cooked
1 cup cheddar cheese	salt and pepper to taste

Melt the butter and whisk in the flour, making a roux. Add to milk, mix well and simmer over low heat for 30 minutes, stirring occasionally. Whisk in the cheese, add truffles and season to taste. Temper the egg with a small amount of cheese sauce, then combine the egg and sauce completely. Add the pasta and mix well.

Mashed Broccoli

4 cups broccoli florets
1/2 stick butter
2 tblsps heavy cream
salt and pepper to taste

Tomato Fondue

2 shallots, minced	1 can diced tomatoes, 15 oz
1 tblsp olive oil	1 tblsp chopped thyme
2 garlic cloves, chopped	salt and pepper to taste

For Mashed Broccoli: Cook broccoli until very soft and drain. Add the butter and cream and whisk until mashed. Season to taste.

For Tomato Fondue: In a sauce pan, sweat the shallots in hot oil for 1 minute. Add the garlic and cook for an additional minute. Mix in tomatoes and thyme. Simmer over low heat for 1/2 hour until thick, with little to no liquid remaining, stirring occasionally. Season to taste.

Balsamic Braised Beef Short Ribs

 Serves four

4 lbs beef short ribs, trimmed
salt and pepper to taste
2 tblsps olive oil
1 carrot, sliced
1 celery stalk, chopped
2 chippolini onions, peeled and diced
2 shallots, chopped

4 garlic cloves, chopped
2 tsps cracked black pepper
2 bay leaves
1 sprig thyme
1/2 cup balsamic vinegar
1 cup red wine
3 cups beef demi glace

Season ribs with salt and pepper, then sear in olive oil until brown. Add the next eight ingredients and saute for 2 to 3 minutes. Stir in the vinegar and wine and simmer until reduced by half. Add the demi glace and braise, covered, in a 375° oven for 1-1/2 to 2 hours, until tender. Sprinkle ribs with gremolata and serve with roasted vegetables.

Gremolata
1 tblsp chopped parsley
mixed with
zest and juice of 1 lemon

Roasted Vegetables
4 carrots, peeled and halved
2 celery stalks, halved
4 plum tomatoes
4 chippolini onions
1 large beet

1 lb fingerling potatoes
3 tblsps chopped thyme
2 garlic cloves, minced
3 tblsps heavy cream
1 tblsp maple syrup
salt and pepper to taste

For Roasted Vegetables: Toss all ingredients together and spread on a sheet tray in a single layer. Roast at 375° for 45 minutes, until vegetables are caramelized.

61

Strip Steak with Mascarpone Creamed Spinach

 Serves four

4 strip steaks, 12 oz each
olive oil
1/4 cup heavy cream
1/4 cup julienned dried apricots
1/4 cup julienned candied ginger
4 cups fresh spinach
1/2 cup mascarpone cheese
salt and pepper to taste

Brush steaks with olive oil and season to taste with salt and pepper. Grill for 4 minutes on each side for medium rare.

In a sauce pan, heat the heavy cream, apricots and ginger and simmer for 1 minute. Before serving, add the spinach and cheese and heat until spinach is just wilted. Salt and pepper to taste.

Chef's Suggestion: Serve with wild mushroom mashed potatoes and fried onion rings.

Grilled Flank Steak & Stuffed Tomatoes

 Serves four

2 lbs flank steak, trimmed
1 tblsp chopped fresh thyme
1 tblsp chopped fresh basil
2 tblsps chopped garlic

1/2 cup red wine
1/4 cup extra virgin olive oil
2 tblsps cracked black pepper
salt to taste

Cut the steak in half lengthwise. Combine remaining ingredients and pat onto steak. Marinate for 45 minutes. Grill for 4 minutes on each side for medium rare. Slice and drizzle with balsamic glaze. Serve with stuffed tomatoes.

Balsamic Glaze
3 tblsps balsamic vinegar
1 cup port

Combine vinegar and port in a sauce pan, cook and reduce until thick.

Stuffed Tomatoes
4 small vine ripe tomatoes
1 tblsp butter
1 tsp minced garlic
1/2 cup heavy cream
1/2 cup shredded white cheddar cheese
2 tblsps bread crumbs

2 cups mixed fresh vegetables
  broccoli florets
  cauliflower florets
  carrots, diced small
  mushrooms, sliced
  asparagus tips
salt and pepper to taste

Blanch tomatoes in boiling water until skins begin to split. Remove from heat and shock in ice water. Remove skin and cut a small slice off the bottom to level. Cut tops off and core, removing all seeds. Melt butter in a saute pan and sweat the garlic. Add the vegetables, heavy cream and cook for 2 minutes. Season with salt and pepper. Add half of the cheese, mix well and cool. Fill each tomato with the mixture, top with remaining cheese and bread crumbs. Bake at 350° for 10 minutes.

Chef's Suggestion: Serve with your favorite mashed potatoes.

Maple Sage Pork Roast

 Serves four

Pork roast, 4 bone-in, frenched
1/4 cup chopped sage
3 tblsps minced garlic
2 tblsps cracked black pepper
1/4 cup maple syrup
salt to taste

Dine at Fred's with the intimate feel of a private club serving grilled meats and entrees including this Maple Sage Pork Roast.

Mix sage, garlic, pepper and maple syrup into a paste and rub on both sides of the roast. Salt to taste. Cover bones with foil and roast at 300° for 1 to 1-1/2 hours. Remove at an internal temperature of 145° and let rest 10 minutes before slicing. Serve with cinnamon vanilla apples and mashed sweet potatoes.

Cinnamon Vanilla Apples
2 tblsps butter
2 Granny Smith apples, diced
1/8 tsp cinnamon
4 tblsps brown sugar
1/2 vanilla bean

Roasted & Mashed Sweet Potatoes
4 medium sweet potatoes
3/4 stick butter
1/8 tsp nutmeg
4 tblsps maple syrup

For Cinnamon Vanilla Apples: Melt the butter in a saute pan, then add the remaining ingredients. Mix well and heat through, stirring occasionally.

For Roasted Sweet Potatoes: Wash and oven roast the potatoes, skin on, until well done. Remove pulp from skin and mix with remaining ingredients. Season to taste.

Pork Tenderloin

Serves four

4 pork tenderloins, 6 oz	1/2 cup sunflower seeds
2 yellow tortilla chips	salt and pepper to taste
1 red tortilla chip	flour
1 blue tortilla chip	1 egg, beaten
1 tblsp chopped thyme	1 tblsp olive oil

In a food processor, chop the tortilla chips, thyme and sunflower seeds together. Salt and pepper the tenderloin, pat with flour then dredge in egg. Coat with the crushed tortilla chip mixture and sear in hot oil on all sides. Finish in a 350° oven for 12 to 15 minutes. Serve with jicama slaw and refried black beans.

Jicama Slaw

3 tblsps malt vinegar	3 tblsps vegetable oil	
3 tblsps honey	1/2 red pepper, julienned	1 ancho chile,
2 tblsps chopped fresh cilantro	1/2 yellow pepper, julienned	rehydrated and julienned
juice of 1 lime	1/2 green pepper, julienned	1/4 medium red onion, julienned
	1/2 jicama, julienned	salt and pepper to taste

Combine all ingredients in a large bowl and mix well.

Refried Black Beans

1 can black beans, 15 oz	1 tblsp chopped garlic
5 bacon slices, chopped	2 tsps cumin
1/2 medium red onion, diced	salt and pepper to taste

Drain and mash black beans. Brown bacon then add onion and garlic. Add cumin, season to taste and mix well with mashed black beans.

Host a foursome or banquet for 300 guests at The Renaissance Vinoy Golf Club, overlooking the newly restored 18-hole championship golf course.

Veal T-Bones with Risotto

Serves four

4 veal t-bones, 12 oz each
3 tblsps olive oil
1 tsp chopped fresh sage
1 tsp chopped fresh basil
1/4 tsp chopped fresh rosemary
2 garlic cloves, minced
1 tblsp cracked black pepper
1 tblsp kosher salt

Green Pea Risotto

2 tblsps olive oil
1/2 medium onion, diced
2 garlic cloves, minced
1 cup Arborio rice
1/4 cup white wine
2-1/2 cups hot chicken broth
1/4 cup heavy cream
1/4 cup grated Romano cheese
1/2 cup fresh green peas
4 tblsps crumbled cooked bacon
salt and pepper to taste

Create a marinade by combining the oil, sage, basil, rosemary and garlic. Cover the t-bones and marinate for 1/2 hour. Season with salt and pepper, then grill for 4 minutes on each side for medium rare.

In a sauce pan, heat oil and sweat the onion and garlic for 1 minute. Add the rice and wine. Cook until the rice has absorbed the wine. Slowly add the hot broth in three divisions, stirring occasionally. Once the broth is absorbed, add the cream, cheese, peas and bacon. Salt and pepper to taste. Remove from heat and serve.

Lamb Chops with Ragout

Celebrate victory and enjoy Lamb Chops with Ragout after a challenging match on the Vinoy's Har-Tru tennis courts.

 Serves four

8 double lamb chops
2 tblsps olive oil
3 garlic cloves, minced
1 tblsp chopped thyme
1 tblsp chopped rosemary
1 tblsp cracked black pepper
1 shallot, minced
1 cup red wine
1-1/2 tblsps whole grain mustard
1 cup demi glace
1 tblsp butter
salt & pepper to taste

Ragout
1/2 tblsp olive oil
6 oz chorizo
1/2 cup pearl onions
8 garlic cloves, slivered
1/2 cup fava beans
1 roasted red pepper, julienned
1 roasted yellow pepper, julienned
1 cup arugula
salt and pepper to taste

Mix the oil, garlic, thyme, rosemary and pepper into a marinade. Place the chops into the marinade for 30 minutes. Season chops with salt and grill for 3 to 4 minutes on each side. For the sauce, put the shallot in a saute pan with wine and reduce by 90% over medium high heat. Whisk in the mustard and demi glace, reduce to a simmer and cook for 10 minutes. Season to taste, remove from heat and add the butter.

For Ragout: Roll the chorizo into little balls and saute in the oil until half cooked. Add the remaining ingredients and saute until the arugula wilts. Season to taste.

Desserts

White Chocolate Cheesecake

Fruit Tarts

Chocolate Macaroons

Fudge Cake

Chocolate Cherry Cake

Macadamia Nut Tart

Creme Brulee

Apple Phyllo

Vinoy's Signature White Chocolate Cheesecake

 Makes one 9" cake

3-1/2 cups soft cream cheese
2 tblsps butter, softened
2/3 cup sugar
1/4 cup heavy cream
1/2 tsp vanilla extract
3 whole eggs
6 oz white chocolate, melted

1/2 cup white chocolate shavings
whipped cream & fresh raspberries to serve

For cake crust:
1-1/2 cups Oreo cake base
2 heaping tblsps flour
2 heaping tblsps sugar

Pastry Chef Bill Hallion shaves white chocolate over his signature cheesecake

In a blender, on low speed, cream together butter, sugar and cream cheese until smooth. Slowly add heavy cream and vanilla, scraping bowl to prevent lumps. Add eggs slowly while scraping and then add chocolate. Meanwhile, combine dry ingredients for crust in mixing bowl and on low speed add the melted butter until combined. Layer bottom of a 9" non-stick baking pan with crust mixture and flatten out firmly. Bake crust for 7 minutes in 325° preheated oven. Remove and let cool. Pour batter into pan over crust. Set pan in water bath and bake at 280° for 1 to 1-1/2 hours until cheesecake sets firm. Chill overnight. Let sit 15 minutes at room temperature, then remove from pan. Coat with whipped cream, chocolate shavings and serve with raspberries.

Fruit Tarts

 Makes four to six tarts

Tart Dough
  1 cup all purpose flour
  1/4 cup cornmeal
  1 tsp sugar
  1/2 tsp salt
  7 tblsps unsalted, cold butter
  3 tblsps sour cream
  5 tblsps ice cold water
  fruit of your choice
  honey
  1/4 cup chopped hazelnuts

Combine flour, cornmeal, sugar and salt in a large bowl. Slice the butter and add to dry ingredients. With a pastry blender or fork, cut the butter into flour mixture until crumbly, about pea size. Whisk the sour cream and water together until smooth and blend half into flour mixture. Blend in remaining half and knead together. Dough will be very sticky. Wrap and refrigerate for at least 3 hours.

Divide dough into 4 to 6 portions. On a floured table, roll each portion out into circles 1/8" thick (a 4" cookie cutter makes a nice circle). On a non-stick or greased cooking sheet, place each circle about 1/2" apart. Place fruit in center, leaving close to 1/2" dough empty around the fruit. Sprinkle with sugar and honey and fold sides up around fruit, pinch to make a rim. Coat rims with chopped nuts. Bake in a preheated 325° oven for 20 to 25 minutes until golden brown.

Chocolate Chip Macaroons

 Makes 3 dozen cookies

5 cups sweet shredded coconut
1/2 cup all purpose flour
1-3/4 cups chocolate chips
1 tblsp rum liqueur
1-3/4 cups sweetened condensed milk

Combine coconut, flour and chips in a mixing bowl. Add milk and rum, then mix on low speed until well combined. Using a tablespoon, scoop mixture and roll into balls and place on a non-stick cookie sheet, leaving 1-1/2" space between each cookie. Preheat oven to 300°and bake for approximately 10 minutes or until light golden brown.

Chocolate Fudge Cake

 Makes one 9" cake

Graham Cracker Crust
1 cup graham cracker crumbs
2 tblsps cake flour
2 tblsps granulated sugar
4 tblsps butter, melted

Fudge Cake
5 tblsps light corn syrup
2-1/3 cups granulated sugar
2 tsps vanilla extract
5 eggs, beaten
3/4 cup butter
1/2 cup dark chocolate, melted

For Graham Cracker Crust: Mix the graham cracker crumbs, flour and sugar together. Add the butter and mix well. Spread on the bottom of a 9" non-stick pan, packing down to cover all of the bottom. Bake at 300° for 5 minutes.

For Fudge Cake: Mix the corn syrup, sugar and vanilla, then add to the beaten eggs. Melt the butter in a sauce pan, whisk in chocolate until well blended, then add to the sugar and egg mixture. Stir well and pour into the graham cracker shell. Bake in a preheated oven at 350° for 35 to 40 minutes until top forms a crust. Cool and serve.

Chef's Suggestion: Serve with strawberry puree, fresh sliced strawberries and top with mint chocolate chip ice cream and chocolate shavings.

Chocolate Amaretto Cherry Cake

 Serves eight

Mousse Filling
2 oz dark chocolate
1/2 cup pastry cream
3/4 cup heavy cream
Amaretto liqueur to taste
pre-baked devil's food cake
Chocolate ganache
40 dark cherries

Chocolate Ganache
10 oz dark chocolate
1/2 cup heavy cream
1/4 cup milk

Pastry Cream
1 cup milk
2 tblsps butter
3 tblsps sugar
1/2 tsp vanilla
1-1/4 tblsps cornstarch
1 egg

For Pastry Cream: Combine 3/4 cup milk with 1-1/2 tblsps sugar, butter and vanilla, then bring to a boil. Remove from heat. Meanwhile, whisk together remaining milk, sugar, cornstarch and eggs. Slowly combine the two mixtures and whisk over medium heat until thick. Remove from heat, cover and chill.

For Mousse Filling: Melt chocolate in a double boiler. Whip pastry cream until smooth and fold into chocolate. Whip heavy cream with hand whisk for 4 minutes until thick and fold into chocolate mixture, making sure not to over mix. Add Amaretto liqueur and blend well.

Cut cake to fit 2-1/2" x 1" dessert molds, two slices per mold. Line bottom of mold with one slice and place 2 cherries in center. Fill with chocolate mixture, top with second cake slice and freeze.

For Chocolate Ganache: Over simmering water, slowly melt chocolate. In a separate pan, bring cream and milk to a boil. Remove from heat and whisk in chocolate until well blended.

To serve, unmold, thaw, then top with chocolate ganache. Garnish with cherries and raspberry sauce.

Macadamia Nut Tarts

 Serves twelve

1 lb macadamia nuts

Sweet Dough
1-1/2 cups butter
1/2 cup plus 1 tblsp sugar
1/2 tsp salt
1 egg, beaten
1-1/2 tblsps vanilla
2-1/4 cups pastry flour

Filling
1/2 cup butter
1-1/2 cups corn syrup
1 cup plus 2 tblsps brown sugar
2 tblsps plus 1 tsp
   all purpose flour
4 eggs, beaten

For Sweet Dough: Cream butter, sugar and salt together. Slowly add egg and vanilla. Add flour and mix until well combined. Refrigerate for at least 6 hours or overnight.

For Filling: Melt butter and corn syrup together. Add sugar and flour, then mix until smooth. Remove from heat and cool completely. Mix in eggs, stirring until smooth.

Roll the dough to 1/8" thick and cut into circles to fit 3-1/2" tart shells. Fill with a single layer of macadamia nuts. Slowly pour the filling over until the nuts are just covered. Bake at 300° to 325° for approximately 20 minutes until golden brown. Let cool and unmold.

Chef's Suggestion: Serve with vanilla ice cream and sliced bananas.

Citrus Creme Brulee

 Serves four

	Tuile Cookies
1 cup heavy cream	1/4 cup sugar
1/2 cup half and half	2 tblsps all purpose flour
5 tblsps sugar	2 egg whites
5 egg yolks	1-1/2 tblsps butter, melted
1/2 tblsp plus 1 tsp orange zest	1/8 tsp vanilla extract
2 oranges or lemons	1/4 cup sesame seeds or
raspberry sauce	crushed pistaschio nuts

The lovely Vinoy Tea Garden is ideal for al fresco dining during weddings and outdoor receptions.

For Creme Brulee: In a sauce pot, bring heavy cream, half and half and orange zest to a boil and remove from heat. In a separate bowl, whisk sugar and egg yolks together. Temper the egg yolks with a little of the hot cream, then add back into remaining cream. Whisk all together. Pour the brulee into an oven safe dish, place in a water bath and bake in a preheated 280°oven for 40 to 50 minutes until set. Cool for 20 minutes, then strain and chill for two hours.

To make fruit cups, place thin slices of oranges or lemons around the sides and bottoms of muffin tins and freeze. Remove the cups and fill with brulee. Sprinkle tops with sugar and caramelize with a brulee torch. Serve with cookies and garnish plates with raspberry sauce.

For Tuile Cookies: Mix sugar, flour and salt together. On low mixer speed, add melted butter and combine well. Thoroughly cool then slowly add egg whites and vanilla. Spread out on well greased sheet pan and sprinkle with sesame seeds or nuts. Bake at 300° for 10 minutes until evenly browned. Remove and, using a pizza cutter, very quickly cut into desired shapes, form and let cool.

Apple Phyllo

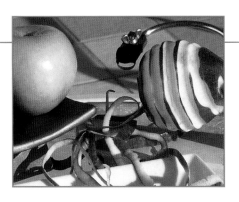

 Makes 3 to 4 rolls

Apple Juice Reduction
  2 cups apple juice
  2 cinnamon sticks
  1 whole clove
  1 vanilla bean
Cook over medium heat and reduce to 1/2 cup.

3 phyllo sheets
1/2 stick butter, melted

Apple Filling
3 tblsps raisins
1-1/2 tblsps brandy
1 granny smith apple
1/4 cup sliced almonds
2 tsps butter
1 tsp apple juice reduction
1 tsp honey
1 tsp cornstarch

For Apple Filling: Soak raisins in brandy for 1/2 hour. Peel and core the apple, slice and cut into 1/4" chunks. Saute apples and almonds in butter until apples are tender. Add the raisins and brandy. Mix the apple juice reduction with the honey and cornstarch to make a slurry. Add slurry to the apples, almonds and raisins and cook over medium heat for 2 minutes until the mixture is tight.

Butter one side of a phyllo sheet with melted butter and sprinkle with sugar. Top with two more sheets with butter and sugar on each. Cut the stack of sheets into thirds. Place the apple filling on the end of each sheet. Fold in the sides and roll. Butter the top of each and sprinkle with sugar. Bake at 350° until golden brown.

Chef's Suggestion: Garnish plates with apricot and blood orange sauces and top with caramel sugar garnish.

Dinner
Party

A glass of Champagne should await each guest at your Vinoy "Simply Elegant" seven course dinner for eight.

Scallop Amuse

Duck & Arugula

Seabass & Lobster

Watermelon Ice

Stuffed Tenderloin

Chocolate Sampler

Cheese Trilogy

Seared Scallops with Rhubarb and Green Apple Relish

 Serves eight

8 large fresh sea scallops
4 oz foie gras, diced
1 cup chicken broth
2 tblsps whole butter
1 tblsp foie gras fat
salt and pepper to taste

Rhubarb and Green Apple Relish
1/8 cup frozen rhubarb
3 tblsps grenadine
1/8 cup small diced Granny Smith apples
2 tblsps butter
2 tblsps Grand Marnier
1 tsp chopped chives
1/4 vanilla bean

Salt and pepper foie gras and sear until fat is rendered. Drain, reserving 1 tblsp fat. Salt and pepper scallops and sear in butter and reserved fat for 1-1/2 minutes on each side. Make a foie gras emulsion by bringing the chicken broth to a boil. Remove from heat and puree with cooked foie gras with a hand blender until foamy.
Serve the scallops over the foie gras emulsion and top with rhubarb and green apple relish.

For Rhubarb and Green Apple Relish: Cook the rhubarb and grenadine until grenadine is absorbed. In a saute pan, sweat the apples in melted butter. Flame with Grand Marnier for 20 seconds. Remove from heat and cool. Add the rhubarb, chives, vanilla bean and mix well.

Wine Recommendation: Pine Ridge Chenin Blanc-Viognier

 Serves eight

Marinated Duck Breast with Arugula

3 duck breasts, 5 oz each
1 tblsp white truffle oil
1 small gherkin
2 tsps chopped parsley
1/2 tsp lemon zest
salt and pepper to taste
2 tblsps canola oil

Arugula with Mustard Oil
2 cups arugula, chiffonade
1 tsp mustard seeds
1/4 cup canola oil
1 tblsp whole grain mustard

Clean and remove all fat from one of the breasts and dice fine. Make a tartare by combining the next five ingredients and mix well. Set aside. Brush the other two breasts with the raspberry beet juice and marinate for 30 to 45 minutes. Sear in canola oil, fat side down first, for 3 minutes on each side. Slice the breasts and serve with arugula and fingerling potatoes topped with tartare.

For Arugula with Mustard Oil: Toast the mustard seeds. In a blender, combine seeds with oil, let sit for 2 hours and strain. Whip in the mustard. Before serving, toss arugula with mustard oil.

Raspberry Beet Juice
1 medium red beet
1/4 cup fresh raspberries
1 tblsp raspberry vinegar

1 tblsp olive oil
1 tsp chopped thyme
1 garlic clove, minced
salt and pepper to taste

Fingerling Potatoes
2 fingerling potatoes
melted butter
salt and pepper to taste

For Raspberry Beet Juice: Skin, blanch and dice beet. Mix all ingredients together and puree.

For Fingerling Potatoes: Slice potatoes paper thin. Place on a cooking sheet lined with parchment paper, brush with butter and season to taste. Top with another sheet of parchment paper, then with another cooking sheet to keep potato slices flat. Bake at 350° for 8 minutes or until golden brown.

Wine Recommendation: Monte Antico Sangiovese, Toscano

Seabass and Lobster
Tangerine Lobster Broth

 Serves eight

8 seabass fillets, 2-1/2 oz each	4 tblsps canola oil	2 garlic cloves, minced
2 Maine lobsters, 1-1/4 lbs each	16 baby carrots	1/4 stick butter
3 tangerines, peeled and juiced	1/2 cup fava beans	salt and pepper to taste
1/2 cup water	1 fennel bulb, shaved	
1/4 cup sugar	16 kalamata olives, pitted	

Cook lobsters in boiling water for 3 to 4 minutes. Clean, remove meat and cut into chunks. Reserve shells for the lobster broth. Peel and juice tangerines, reserving juice for the lobster broth. Cook the tangerine skins in water and sugar for 5 minutes. Drain and bake at 250° for 15 to 20 minutes until crisp. Grind in a blender. Coat the seabass with the tangerine dust and sear in oil for 3 minutes per side. Melt butter and saute the carrots, beans, fennel, olives and garlic. Add the lobster meat and salt and pepper to taste. Place the vegetables in a shallow bowl, top with a fillet of fish and pour broth over.

Tangerine Lobster Broth	1/2 rib of celery	1 qt water
shells from lobsters, above	1/4 cup tomato paste	1 sprig of fresh dill
2 whole garlic cloves	1/4 cup sherry	1/4 stick butter
1/2 carrot	1/2 cup white wine	salt and pepper to taste
1/2 onion	juice of tangerines, above	

Saute shells in a hot 4 quart sauce pan. Add garlic, carrot, onion, celery and saute 2 minutes. Add the tomato paste, sherry, wine, tangerine juice and reduce until thick and pasty. Cover with water, add dill and simmer for 30 to 45 minutes. Strain, whisk in butter, salt and pepper to taste.

Wine Recommendation: Chateau St. Jean Chardonnay, Sonoma

Fresh Watermelon Ice

 Serves eight

1/4 cup sugar
1/2 cup water
1-1/2 cups seedless
watermelon chunks
2 tblsps watermelon Schnapps
4 oz vodka

Crystallized Melon Rind
1-1/2 cups julienned
melon rind
1/2 cup sugar
2 tblsps water

Combine sugar and water and bring to a boil. Remove from heat and cool. Cover and refrigerate for 4 hours.

Puree watermelon chunks in a blender for 1 minute. Add the sugar water, Schnapps and mix for 30 seconds. Freeze for 3 hours until firm.

Remove from freezer, shave with a fork and beat at medium speed with a mixer for one minute until light and fluffy. Cover and freeze for 4 hours.

For Crystallized Melon Rind: Place all ingredients in saute pan and cook over medium heat. Remove from heat just before sugar caramelizes and immediately spread out on wax paper. Let cool.

Serve ice in martini glasses and drizzle vodka over each. Garnish with crystallized melon rind.

Stuffed Tenderloin Morel Sauce

Serves eight

1 lb chateau tenderloin, cut into quarters lengthwise

1-1/2 lbs veal loin

2 tblsps chiffonade basil

2 tblsps chopped thyme

3 garlic cloves, minced

1 tblsp cracked black pepper

salt to taste

3 tblsps olive oil

Butterfly veal, pound flat and cut into four squares. Mix basil, thyme, garlic, pepper and rub over all sides of both meats. Season with salt. Place beef quarter on veal square, roll tight and tie. Sear in oil until just brown. Roast at 350° for 8 minutes to an internal temperature of 120°. Let rest 5 minutes. Cut each piece into four slices, serve with morel sauce, asparagus and onion marmalade.

Morel Sauce

1/4 cup dried morels

1 shallot, minced

1/2 cup Merlot

1 cup demi glace

2 tblsps butter, softened

salt and pepper to taste

Onion Marmalade

1/2 onion, diced fine

1/4 cup red wine

1 tblsp balsamic vinegar

2 tblsps grenadine

For Morel Sauce: Rehydrate morels in water, drain then slice. In a sauce pot, cook morels, shallot, wine and reduce until almost dry. Add demi and simmer 20 minutes. Stir in butter and season.

For Onion Marmalade: Combine all ingredients in sauce pan and reduce until dry. Season and chill.

Asparagus with Truffle Bean Puree

2 lbs asparagus

1 can cannellini beans, 15 oz

3 tblsps heavy cream

1 tblsp chopped black truffles

salt and pepper to taste

Drain beans and puree in food processor with the cream. Combine truffles and puree, season and heat until hot. Cut the asparagus into 3" spears and blanch in water. In a 2" cylinder mold, stack asparagus and pipe bean puree into the middle. Remove the mold and serve.

Wine Recommendation: Greg Norman Cabernet-Merlot, Limestone Coast

White Chocolate Creme Brulee Chocolate Molten Cake

Serves eight

Chocolate Molten Cake

3 egg yolks
1/4 cup water
1 cup dark chocolate, melted

1/4 cup melted butter
1/4 cup all purpose flour
1 tblsp corn starch
1 tblsp cocoa powder
1 tsp cream of tartar

1/2 cup egg whites
1/2 cup sugar
8 ganache balls
vanilla ice cream
8 sesame tuile cookies

Whip egg yolks with water until foamy. Combine the chocolate with the butter and add to the egg mix. Sift flour, corn starch and cocoa powder together and fold into the chocolate egg mixture. Whip the egg whites with cream of tartar until soft, then slowly whip in the sugar until stiff. Fold into chocolate egg mixture.

Using the recipe on page 85, make the ganache, chill, roll into small balls and freeze. Spray eight timbales (4 oz stainless steel cups) and fill to 1/4 full with molten mix. Top each with a ganache ball then fill to 3/4 full with molten mix. Bake at 300° for 15 minutes or until crust forms on top. Cool for 1 hour. Unmold and garnish with vanilla ice cream and a sesame tuile cookie (recipe on page 89).

White Chocolate Raspberry Creme Brulee

1 cup heavy cream
1/2 cup half and half
5 tblsps sugar

5 egg yolks
2/3 cup white chocolate, diced small
1 pint fresh raspberries

Use creme brulee method on page 89. After heating cream, remove from heat and add white chocolate instead of zest. Place a spoonful of brulee into each of eight 2 oz ceramic egg cups. Put two raspberries into each cup and fill with brulee. Sprinkle tops with sugar and caramelize with a brulee torch. Garnish with white chocolate and fresh raspberries.

Wine Recommendation: Bonny Doon Framboise

Cheese Trilogy

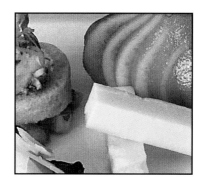

Serves eight

Pecorino with Honey Roasted Plums
4 small black plums
1/4 cup honey
4 oz Pecorino cheese

Halve and pit plums and place on a cookie sheet lined with wax paper. Drizzle with honey and roast at 350° for 10 to 15 minutes until caramelized and soft. Chill and top with shaved pecorino cheese.

Sharp White Vermont Cheddar with Poached Pears
8 oz sharp white Vermont cheddar cheese
8 baby pears, peeled
3 cups red wine

1 cup water
1/4 cup sugar
1 cinnamon stick

Combine the wine, water, sugar and cinnamon stick. Bring to a boil, add pears, and simmer 4 minutes. Remove from heat and cool. Cut the cheese into 1/2″ x 1-1/2″ sticks. Drain the pears, fan and serve with cheese sticks.

Roquefort with Apricots and Baguettes
3 fresh small apricots, diced
1 tblsp butter
2 tsps sugar

2 oz brandy
1 tsp chopped tarragon
8 slices sour dough baguette, 1/4″ thick
8 oz Roquefort

Melt the butter and sweat the apricots for 30 seconds. Add the sugar and flame with brandy. Let cool and add tarragon. Divide apricots and top with a slice of bread. Finish with Roquefort cheese.

Wine Recommendation: Fonseca Bin 27 Reserve Porto

Glossary

&

Index

GLOSSARY

BALSAMIC REDUCTION
Balsamic vinegar that has been reduced in a sauce pot by two-thirds and cooled. It has the texture of syrup.

BRULEE TORCH
A small butane torch used for caramelizing sugar. It can be found in specialty cooking stores such as William Sonoma.

CANDIED GINGER
Fresh ginger that has been cooked in sugar until crystallized. It can be found in Asian markets.

CARAMEL SUGAR GARNISH
Granulated sugar mixed with water and cooked until caramel colored, slightly cooled then shaped into desired garnish.

CHIFFONADE
Very finely shredded or sliced vegetables or herbs, such as basil, lettuce or arugula.

CRYSTALLIZED
Sugar cooked and removed from heat just as it starts to turn caramel brown.

DEMI GLACE
A rich brown sauce that begins with veal stock reduced by half, used as a base for many sauces. It can be purchased in your grocery store.

EMULSION
To slowly add one ingredient to another while mixing rapidly.

FOIE GRAS ("Fat Liver")
The enlarged liver from a duck or goose that has been force fed over several months. Weight is between 1 and 3 pounds. Use in mousses, pates or sauces, either sauteed, seared or grilled.

NORI
Paper thin sheets of dried seaweed, generally used for wrapping sushi or rice balls. It can be found in Asian markets.

PAELLA
A Spanish dish made with saffron flavored rice combined with a variety of meats and shellfish. It is named after the special two-handled pot that is also called paella.

PHYLLO
Tissue-thin layer of pastry dough used in various sweet and savory dishes. It can be found in the frozen section of your grocery store.

POTATO PAVE
A layered potato dish with heavy cream, eggs and cheese that is baked and cut into squares.

SWEAT
To cook vegetables in butter or oil until their flavor is released.

SLURRY
Cornstarch mixed with a liquid.

TARTARE
Coarsely ground or finely chopped high-quality lean meat, seasoned with salt, pepper and herbs. Served raw.

TEMPER
To balance the temperature of a cool ingredient with a little of a hot ingredient before adding it to the whole of the hot ingredient. Prevents curdling and separation.

WATER BATH (Bain Marie)
To place a container of food into another larger container in which warm water surrounds the food with gentle heat. Use this method to cook delicate dishes such as custards, mousses and cheesecakes.

INDEX

INDEX

*The Vinoy wishes to thank all the masterful chefs
whose knowledge and contributions made this book possible,
especially Executive Chef John Pivar,
Executive Sous Chef Mark Heimann,
Pastry Chef Bill Hallion and Banquet Chef James Samson.*

First Published in U.S.A in 2004 by Espichel Enterprises

*Managing Editor: Susan Eanes
Food Director: Chef John Pivar
Food Preparation: Chef Mark Heimann, Bill Hallion
Design & Photography: Charles Eanes*

*Library of Congress Control Number: 2004090618
ISBN 1-890494-09-7*

Printed in the USA

*RENAISSANCE VINOY RESORT
AND GOLF CLUB
501 Fifth Avenue, N.E., St. Petersburg, Florida 33701
727/894-1000 ~ TDD 727/821-7010 ~ FAX 727/822-2785
www.renaissancehotels.com/TPASR*